Caution! God at Work

Trusting God Through Tough Times

Bishop Timothy J. Clarke

Caution: God at Work: Trusting God Through Tough Times
Copyright © 2010 by Timothy J. Clarke
First Printing: September 2012

ISBN 978-0-9764022-5-1

Powerful Purpose Publishing Company
P O Box 32132, Columbus, OH 43232

Publishing Consultant: Obieray Rogers (www.rubiopublishing.com)

Printed in the United States of America

Table of Contents

From time to time every preacher finds themselves asking the age-old question of what shall I preach? The genesis of that question is not found in the scarcity of preaching material, but rather a desire on the part of the preacher to meet a real need in the life of the worshiper. The preacher's goal is for those who sit under their preaching to be confronted and comforted by the claims and promises of God.

I suppose in some ways those of us who preach the Gospel can find comfort in knowing that we are not the first to raise this question. In fact, the question is as old as the prophet Isaiah: *"A voice says, 'cry out.' And I said, 'What shall I cry?'"* (Isaiah 40:6), which only goes to show that even the prophet occasionally found himself stymied as to what he should preach. I have to confess that after preaching for over thirty-five years that every now and then I find myself wondering, "What can I say that I haven't already said?" and the answer came to me as I was rummaging through the Word of God.

All of us have seen those signs that read, "Caution: People at Work," which serve as a reminder for us to slow down, be more alert and aware because there are men and women on the road working. You may be upset that you have to slow down because they are working, but what you have to remember is that they are working for your good. I hate seeing the orange barrels because they usually mean that it is going to take longer for me to reach my destination. I have to slow down for a temporary inconvenience while people are working on a permanent improvement. Sometimes the road work is hidden behind a canopy and you can't see what is going on.

You must understand that while God may have you slowing down, and while you may not be making the progress that you want to make, you can still celebrate the fact that God is at work. And if God is working, He is always working for your good, even when you cannot see it.

Caution: God at Work is meant to bring hope to Christians who find themselves in difficult situations or dealing with some painful fact or reality in their life. This book is meant to remind you that no matter what you face, or what you go through, there is never a time when God is not at work in you and never a time when God is not at work on your behalf. In fact, beloved, right now while you are hurting, right now while your heart is breaking, right now in the midst of your pain and your questions, God is at work.

PART ONE

GOD AT WORK
IN THE MIDST OF DEVASTATION

Chapter One:
God, The Re-Creator

How you see God is one of the most important things about you. So before we go any further allow me to ask a question: What is your view and concept of God? The Bible tells us that one of the profiles we should have of God is that of a worker. I know we may struggle with that particular image of God because we are told (and I believe it is true) that everything God created was done with words from His mouth. In fact, the only thing that God touched in creation was man and woman when He made them in His image and after His likeness. God spoke the rest of creation into existence; yet, with the absence of sweat and contact, God was still working. Everything we see in creation—from the blazing sun to the lilies of the field; the snow-capped peaks of Switzerland, the lush jungles of Africa, the foggy bogs of Scotland; the birds of the air and the blades of grass on your front yard—were all made by God.

The beauty and greatness of God's power is not just seen in His creative power; what is really worth celebrating is the God who *re*-creates. The prefix "re" means to go back to your original state. We serve a God who can take something that had been messed up and create a miracle. If your world is spiraling and spinning out of control because of devastation, death, debt, divorce, disappointment, disease, or despair, God is at work re-creating your world in the midst of your deepest devastation. You are rocking and reeling from the blows of devastation that have swept over your life and you are wondering if God is working. Hold on, help is on the way! Just like we send rescue workers to places that are devastated, God sends the Holy Ghost as His agent of rescue.

Some of you are dealing with a devastating experience that has shaken you to your core and the question you are asking is: Will I ever be able to come back from this or is this my death warrant? I want you to know this is not your burial. We are not ready to commit you earth-to-earth, ashes-to-ashes and dust-to-dust. We came to have a party, a celebration, because you are about to rise and not die.

You may be dealing with the devastation of sickness where you have just received a diagnosis and prognosis that has utterly wiped you out. You may be dealing with a financial devastation where your portfolio has taken such a hit that you don't know whether you can afford to retire. You may be dealing with the devastation of divorce; the person you gave your body, heart, and soul to left you and you are now trying to pull the pieces of your emotional life back together. You may be dealing with the devastation of death and you have asked the question "Where is God?" You may be dealing with the devastation of the disappointment of a child who has broken your heart as only a child can. Or it may be the fear of getting older in a world that doesn't honor and respect older people. Everyone is dealing with devastation on some level. But the God we serve does His best work in a devastated environment.

ONE MAN AND A BOAT

How do I know that the God we serve is not just a creator but a re-creator? Because I have read the Bible and the story of Noah and the ark reinforces my belief in God the re-creator:

> *But God remembered Noah and all the animals in the boat. . . After another forty days, Noah opened the window he had made in the boat and released a raven that flew back and forth until the earth was dry. Then he sent out a dove to see if it could find dry ground. But the dove found no place to land because the water was still too high. So it returned to the*

7

boat, and Noah held out his hand and drew the dove back inside. Seven days later, Noah released the dove again. This time, toward evening, the bird returned to him with a fresh olive leaf in its beak. Noah now knew that the water was almost gone. A week later, he released the dove again, and this time it did not come back. (Genesis 8:1, 6-12, NLT)

Genesis chapter eight takes place after the flood that brought devastation to the world. God wiped everything out and started the creation process over. In the midst of devastation, God brought order and a new creation. God is so much God, and His rebuilding skills are so great, that He can rebuild right where the devastation takes place.

There are some of you who in the last few months have seen almost everything you have devastated—your health, your finances, your relationships—but you don't need to give up, because the God you serve is one who steps into the midst of devastation and works a new creation. God will start working all over again.

That is good news for those of you who have been contemplating pulling up stakes and leaving town because the pressure is too much for you. Losing your job, your husband walking out, your wife being unfaithful, financial setbacks have proven too much for you, so you have already decided to start your life all over again. Save your money and rebuild right where you are with God's help. You can stay and stand right where you are, because God is at work rebuilding your life right where the devastation took place. God keeps us in the place we would rather leave and rebuilds our lives at the site of the devastation for the following reasons:

- He wants to use you as a reference. God will leave you in a devastating place and rebuild your life right there so that when somebody else is going through devastation, He can use you as a reference.

- He wants to use you as a reminder to others. There are some situations that God puts us in, and puts us through, so that out of it He can use us as Exhibit A of His sustaining power. God wants you to be a visual reminder that if He did it for you, He will do the same thing for them.

God waited until the flood was over before starting the task of rebuilding. He allowed the waters to recede before beginning the clean-up process. This is a truth for people dealing with devastation that I don't want you to miss. You have to get some stuff cleaned up before the work can begin.

Several years ago my wife and I had a terrible flood in our home that damaged our entire lower level. The contractor worked all night getting the water out of our basement and we set stuff back in place. The following morning we discovered more water and the process had to begin all over again. We realized that when the contractor came to extract the water the first time, he only addressed the visible signs of the problem. The point of entry for the water was never shut off so the first clean-up was a waste of time and money. Within twenty-four hours the water entered back in at the original point of entry. My wife and I had to throw just about everything away that was in our lower level, but it would have been silly to try to hold onto damaged stuff.

The same is true in our lives. There are some things we want God to fix and work on but God says, "No, I am not going to waste my time until you deal with the point of entry." So that means you have to go to work on yourself so that God's work is not a waste of time. God cannot work on your marriage, your money, or your ministry until you deal with certain issues. We want God to hurry up and get to work, but He is not going to because He knows that if He cleans it up today, within twenty-four hours it is going to be a mess again. It is only when you get the stuff out of the way that God steps in and starts working.

God started with a few people, but keep in mind that people are why God sent the flood in the first place: *"But Noah found favor in the eyes of the Lord,"* (Genesis 6:8). When God was ready to go to work and rebuild the world, He started with people and employed Noah as the construction foreman for His rebuilding enterprise. God spared Noah and allowed him to work with Him to start all over.

You may need to slow down, calm down, and realize that God is at work. While the devil may have told you that you are through, God told me to tell you that He is not through with you. Some of you are worried about being too old to get a new job because you have been laid off. You are not too old or too washed up. If you are still alive, it means that God has kept you alive for a reason. So what if you are older? All that means is that you are smarter now that you have ever been in your life. You know more now than you ever knew before. You have been through more than you have been through before. But here is what you need to get excited about: You have been through it all and you survived. You didn't lose your mind and end up in a padded cell or in a straight jacket. Yes, it was tough, but you survived. Yes, it was difficult, but you came through it. If God brought you through, it is because God wants to use you to start all over. Your best days are ahead of you!

- You can ride out your devastation no matter how long it takes. Latch on, dig in, and hold onto God to ride out the flood. God didn't let Noah die, drown, and get taken over by the devastation.

- The ark was a boat, not a submarine; no matter how high the water rose, the ark stayed afloat. That tells me that the thing you fear the most is the very thing God is going to use to lift you up.

You serve a God who will take you around the pitfalls of your enemy and allow you to rise above the devastation. If you ride it out, you will rise above it. If you rise above it, your ending will be better than your beginning. The God we serve does His best work in a devastated environment.

Chapter Two:
In The Midst of Your Trials

The power of God is not just seen in God's ability to create; but the real power of God is seen in His ability to re-create. We all know that God is the Creator. We know that God stood in the middle of nowhere, on the platform of nothing, and spoke worlds into existence. But what we often miss (and we miss it to our detriment especially when we are going through), is that God is also a re-creator. The same God that takes nothing and makes something is the same God that can step into the middle of a mess and bring a miracle out of it.

It is one thing to serve a God who can stand on pristine ground and make a world out of clean, fresh, never-been-used stuff. But sometimes I need a God who can roll up His sleeve, stick His hand in the mess and muck that I have made, and bring some good out of it.

I am glad that God made the world and that after the flood He re-made the world. What that means is that if God can re-make *the* world, He can re-make *my* world. I don't just serve a God who makes worlds spin in trifocal and centrifugal motion on their axis. I serve a God who gets in my world and when life has messed up my world, He re-creates it.

GOD IS AT WORK IN THE DEVASTATION YOU DID NOT CAUSE

When God was ready to destroy the earth, God found one man who was the great exception: Noah. The Bible says that Noah found favor in the eyes of God, which means that while everybody else was living a wicked life, Noah was living righteous. Noah wasn't living wicked, but God destroyed the world because of wickedness. Noah's world still got turned upside down over something that wasn't his fault.

That might be your story. You did everything you could and your life still went crazy. You took care of your spouse and they still walked out. You worked hard and they still fired you. You exercised and ate right and you still got cancer. You are dealing with devastation you didn't cause and that is what makes devastation so devastating. Sometimes you are made to deal with stuff that is not your fault. So how does God help you deal with the devastation you didn't cause?

- By preparing you. Before the flood came God gave Noah time to get himself and his family ready. Are you willing to admit that even though you may be experiencing devastation you didn't cause, before it came God started doing stuff to get you ready for it? He is doing that for you right now, because He has you reading this book in preparation so that when the devastation comes you won't be overwhelmed. God will never send anything in your life without prior preparation. He will give you warning and prepare you. He will start dealing with you about certain things in advance. And that is the only reason you won't lose your mind when you experience devastation.

- By providing for you. God provided Noah with an ark, which means that He will shut you in to keep out what is messing with everybody else. Not only has God prepared you, but in the midst of your devastation He is providing for you. You wonder how you are making it. This is how: Every day God is giving you strength, courage, hope, grace, peace, and joy. He is giving you a song or a Scripture or something to hold onto in the midst of the devastation.

- By protecting you. What blesses me about Noah and the ark is that Noah rode *out* and rode *on* what killed everybody else! Noah was safe in the ark that God provided so that He could protect him while the storm was raging. You are in a place in your life that is similar to a butterfly in a cocoon. You are wrapped up in the secretions and the web so that while you are in the cocoon, you are covered and protected until it is time for you to come out. You have gone through so much that you should have lost your mind, but God has wrapped you up and kept you safe in the midst of the devastation.

GOD IS AT WORK IN THE DEVASTATION YOU CANNOT CONTROL

Noah didn't cause the world's devastation, but neither could he control it. If he could have stopped the flood he would have, but there are some things that God takes out of our control.

Remember the cocoon I just referenced? I remember a story from years ago—it may be true or it may be an allegory, but it has a powerful principal nevertheless—about a little boy who saw a butterfly wrestling to break out of the cocoon. Wanting to spare the butterfly the struggle, he opened the cocoon for the butterfly to fly away. Three times the butterfly flapped its wings and three times the butterfly failed. The little boy looked at the butterfly and said, "Fly. I let you out." His father said, "That's the worst thing you could have done. The struggle to break free is what builds up the butterfly's muscles so it can fly. No struggle, no fight. No fight, no flight." Sometimes in our desperation to help people we take them out of the struggle that gives them strength. God takes some things out of our control because He knows it will make us better.

- God supervises what you are going through. God is moving and rearranging stuff. He is pulling some people out of your life and bringing other people into your life. He is closing one door and opening another. He is rearranging your furniture and redirecting your path, and all of it is His supervisory work in the midst of your devastating experience.

- God sustains you while you are going through. When you are getting weak and can't take anymore, God comes along and sustains you so that in the midst of your weakness, God is your strength. The only reason you are making it is because day after day after day God is sustaining you. If it wasn't for God, you would have fallen apart a long time ago. Every time you are about to

17

collapse, God holds you up. Every time you are about to go to pieces, God holds you up. His sustaining power is keeping you in the midst of it all.

GOD IS AT WORK IN THE DEVASTATION YOU COULD NEVER HAVE CONCEIVED

One thing that makes devastation so devastating is that in your wildest dreams you could never have imagined what you are going through. When God wiped out the world with a flood, Noah had no frame of reference for comparison. Noah had never seen rain before, let alone a flood! Nothing had ever come down from the sky because God watered the earth with a midst that came up from the ground. Noah could never have conceived rain.

Some of you are walking through things today that you could never have conceived. In fact, if somebody had told you last year that you would be going through what you are going through, you would have told them they were crazy. You couldn't imagine what they were talking about and that is why you are devastated. So how do you handle it? By remembering these three things:

- God is determining the devastation. What does that mean? God lets nothing come into your life that He has not already inspected and has made three determinations about it: You are coming out; you are coming out better than you went in, and you will be able to bless someone else because of what you went through. As long as you understand that God is working to determine the outcome, you don't have to worry.

- God is directing the devastation. Just like a choir director determines who sings what and when; when the song starts and when the song finishes, the beat and the rhythm et cetera, God is directing your life determining who is coming in and who is going out and how long things are going to last. He is the ultimate choir director.

- God is defining the devastation. That means that we must be careful who we give the power of definition to because some of us have allowed the wrong people to define us. Because you are a woman, you can't do this. Because you are a certain race, you can't do that. Because you are old, you can't do this or that. We have allowed people to define our lives, but there is only One who has the power of definition and that is your Maker. You should refuse to let people define you because then they will want to confine you.

They will want to determine how far you can go, what you can get, and who you will be.

Your destiny is in the hands of God, not people. You need to make up your mind right now that you are coming out of your devastation alive. You thought you weren't going to make it, but you will. You thought you wouldn't be able to come back, but you will. God is at work in the midst of your devastation to make sure you survive.

Chapter Three:
It Is Never Too Late For God

I am excited to serve a God who can step in the middle of chaos and mess and bring life and order out of it. That is a good reason to praise Him! God doesn't just work in creation, but He does His best work in re-creation. He doesn't just order the world; He re-orders the world.

After the flood, the only thing left on the earth is the ark with Noah and his family inside. When God originally made the world, it was perfect. He created man and woman and said, *"Be fruitful, multiple and have dominion."* Man allowed sin to mar God's creation—paradise lost—but thanks be to God for the second Adam, Jesus Christ, who got us out of trouble. The first Adam messed us up, but the second Adam saved us. The first Adam plunged us into sin, but the second Adam brought us salvation. The first Adam caused us to lose everything, but we got it all back with the second Adam. Paradise lost with the first Adam; paradise regained with the second Adam.

A NARROW VIEW OF GOD

J. B. Phillips in his book, *Your God is Too Small,* argues that we have miniaturized the Christian God in America to such a point that we have made Him in our image, when in reality He made us in His image. In other words, God looks more like us rather than us striving to look more like Him. Nothing in our human frame of reference will allow us to fully compute this. Remember the television series, *Lost in Space?* When someone said something that the robot didn't understand, the robot would respond with, "That does not compute." We could say the same about our understanding of God. We reach a point where our theology breaks down and like Paul we can only say, *"Beyond all question, the mystery of godliness is great,"* (1 Timothy 3:16(a)).

God is a tremendous mystery; God doesn't need anything or anybody. He is self-contained, self-sufficient, and self-adequate by Himself, but some of us think He became God in Genesis 1:1. He was God way before that, which is why there is a Genesis 1:1. He was fully God in the beginning before the beginning began. There is not a God because there was a beginning; there is a beginning because there is a God.

I mentioned this only to prove my point that God didn't need our permission to re-create the world. When I get to heaven, I am going to ask God why He thought people would get it right the second time. What a risk our God took. But He took a risk with Adam like He takes a risk on us every day when He wakes us up and gives us free reign and volition. Many times we turn away from God, and yet His grace and mercy watches over us.

God re-created the world with Noah, his family, and two of each animal because it doesn't take much for God to work things out. That shouldn't surprise us because He originally started with less than that. He re-created the world and started the process of orderly re-creation. Why? I'm so glad you asked.

GOD WILL NOT ALLOW HIS NAME TO BE DEFAMED

Remember when God was going to wipe out the children of Israel and Moses interceded on their behalf? Moses told God He couldn't wipe them out because it would make Him look bad. His enemies would say that He took the Israelites out of Egypt, but couldn't take them into the Promised Land so He killed them to save His reputation. Moses told God that His name was on the line, and if He didn't bring the children of Israel into the Promised Land, He would be the one to look bad, not them (Exodus 32).

Timothy J. Clarke

I want you to know that whatever you are going through ceased being about you months ago, because now God is in the fight and His name is on the line, not yours. He is not going to let His name go down. The only thing God honors more than His name is His Word. He is not going to let His name fail, because if that happens then His Word isn't any good, and if His Word isn't any good then His name is no good. He is going to fight for His name and His Word because they are both on the line.

GOD WILL NOT ALLOW YOU
TO BE DESTROYED

The flood could not and did not destroy Noah, and neither will what you are going through destroy you. God will not allow this devastation to destroy you. I know the devil told you it would, but he is a liar and you need to stop listening to him.

If you have ever observed the United Nations either televised or in person, you will notice that when people speak to the General Assembly everyone has on a set of headphones. Someone is interpreting what the speaker is staying into a language that the listener can understand. Every now and then you need a spiritual interpreter because anytime the devil talks to you he is lying, which means that you need to reverse whatever he is saying to you. This is how it works: The devil says,

"You are not going to make it," but God interprets that to say, "You *are* going to make it!" If the devil says you can't, God says you can. If the devil says you won't, God says you will. The only time you need to be concerned is when the devil makes you think that everything is all right. Now, since you know he is a liar that means that all hell is getting ready to break loose! Even so, God is with you no matter what happens and you will be able to handle whatever is coming your way.

GOD WILL NOT ALLOW SATANIC DEVICES TO WIN

The reason God sent the flood in the first place was because of sin which is authored by Satan. If God had left the world in devastation, then that would have meant that the plans of Satan for the world had succeeded. The devil slithered up to Eve to pull a coup d'état on God. Adam and Eve plunged us into sin which brought the world's cosmic order under the control of Satan (which is why the Bible calls him the prince of the power of this world order, Ephesians 2:2). That does not mean that Satan is in control of the world; he is not! The devil doesn't care about us; we are merely pawns in his efforts to get to God. For God to leave the world devastated would have been to buy into the plan and strategy of the devil.

The devil actually thought that sin had won because he had gotten to Adam and Eve and God was destroying the world. It appeared that sin had won, but God remembered Noah. God laughed to Himself and said, "Obviously, the devil didn't have his eye on the ark because I have reserved some people that I can use to start over. I am not going to let his devices succeed." God let Satan know that He was still in charge.

One of the reasons I know that you are going to come out of your devastation with your life rebuilt is because the devastation was the result of satanic action, and God is never going to let Satan win. The devil is betting that he will be able to get you so far out of God's will that you will never be able to get back, but what you have to remember is that it doesn't matter how far you go, God can go there and get you back.

I just need you to be willing not to throw in the towel. The worst thing you can do is give into the devastation, because then you will have co-signed the devil's devices. If you can remember that God is not going to let Satan win, then you can rebuke the devil and start believing that God is going to bring you out. God has an eviction notice ready for the devil, and He is getting ready to rebuild your life and take you to an entirely new level in Him.

PART TWO

GOD AT WORK
IN THE MIDST OF DESTRUCTION

Chapter Four:
Strength to Begin Again

I have often said that it is far more difficult to begin again rather than to begin. To begin again speaks to work already done and efforts already made. In most cases when a person has to begin again, the work already done and the effort already made seems to have resulted in that which is unrewarded and most often unrealized. To begin again is to suggest by its very nature that something has gone wrong, and that no matter how far along the work has progressed for some reason the task must start all over again:

> *Speak to Zerubbabel son of Shealtiel, governor of Judah, to Joshua son of Je-hozadak, the high priest and to the rem-nant of the people. Ask them, 'Who of you is left who saw this house in its former glory? How does it look to you now? Does it not seem to you like nothing?'* (Haggai 2:2-3)

Darius, the king of Persia, had issued a decree that all foreigners who had been brought to Babylon (or any part of the Persian Empire) could return to their own land. These people represented the Diaspora—Jews scattered throughout Babylon and Persia—who returned to the land of Israel and left behind years of captivity and bondage. Once they returned home they began to resettle back into the patterns of life by building houses, gardens, vineyards, and cultivating their fields. Yet, the temple remained in ruins. What was once the center of their lives, the essence of who they were, was desolated and deserted, and it seemed as if they had no energy to begin the task of rebuilding the temple.

These people found themselves in the strange and unwelcome place of beginning again. Like most of us, they had come to that place and struggle, as we often do, of picking up the pieces and starting all over again. In fact, chapter one of Haggai suggests that they had been avoiding rebuilding and it took a Word from God, via the prophet, to get them back on task:

> *So the Lord sent this message through the prophet Haggai: Why are you living in luxurious houses while my house lies in ruins? This is what the Lord Almighty says: Consider how things are going for*

you! You have planted much, but harvested little. You have food to eat, but not enough to fill you up. You have wine to drink, but not enough to satisfy your thirst. You have clothing to wear, but not enough to keep you warm. Your wages disappear as though you were putting them in pockets filled with holes! This is what the Lord Almighty says: Consider how things are going for you! Now go up into the hills, bring down timber, and rebuild my house. Then I will take pleasure in it and be honored, says the Lord.
(Haggai 1:3-8, NLT)

They discover—and this is the good news that we need to hold onto—that even in the midst of having to rebuild, God was at work with them in the rebuilding just like He was in the building.

The Book of Haggai speaks to all of us who have ever had the job, task, assignment, or hard work of rebuilding or starting over again. Or who has had the hard work of putting back together something that has been destroyed. This is the issue I want to examine in this chapter. I want us to realize that the God we serve is a God who is busy at work with us as we seek to rebuild our lives after something we love has been destroyed.

Some of us can admit that there are some things in our lives we are trying to put back together, but the destruction has been so great until we are not sure we even have the energy to start working again. If you have been avoiding or dreading the challenge of rebuilding after something in your life has been destroyed, then this chapter is for you.

The temple which had been such a big part of the lives and history of the Jews had been destroyed when Babylon sacked the city of Jerusalem. Now this people must work to put things back into place and rebuild what had been destroyed by others.

GOD HELPS YOU START OVER
IN THE MIDST OF YOUR PAIN

With one question—*"Who of you is left who saw this house in its former glory?"*—God went to the heart of the issue: Dealing with the pain of loss. The house that God referred to was the temple of Solomon, which is still considered one of the great wonders of the world. It was known for its beauty, glory, splendor, and architectural genius.

Beloved, one thing that makes starting over so hard is we have to deal with the pain of what we have lost. If you have ever suffered loss in your life, then you know how hard it is to pick up the pieces and deal with putting things back together while still feeling the pain of what you lost. Life is filled with loss, and loss always brings pain.

I understood this several years ago when a friend of mind, Bishop Joey Johnson, did a grief counseling session for my staff. Bishop Johnson talked about how painful loss is and then he said that there was such a thing as the loss of a less-than-loved one. I questioned what that was and Bishop Johnson used this example: A couple goes through a contentious divorce and then one of them passes away. The Church never deals with the grief that person feels, because we think that for the person to lose the ex-spouse is a relief, but that is not true. Even losing someone you had a bad experience with will sometimes cause you to wonder what you could have done to make things better.

What I am trying to tell you is that life is filled with loss and every loss has pain whether it is the loss of a business, career, relationship, or confidence. The memory of how and why it was lost is always painful. You might be dealing with a loss in your life and trying to act like it doesn't bother you, but loss is always painful. No matter what the loss is, where the loss is, or how the loss comes about, there is good news for you:

- God considers the loss. How do I know? Because in helping Israel deal with their pain, He raised the question that produced the pain: *"Who is among you that remembers how it used to be?"* We wish we could make things like they were. We wish we could turn back the hands of time. We wish we could reverse the process that has gotten us to where we are. One of the things we struggle with is how to deal with our current reality and still remember the pleasure of how it used to be.

- God cares about the loss. We live in a world where folks are very impatient and they want you to get over whatever you are going through as quickly as possible. You can lose someone you love and people want you to grieve about a week and then they are encouraging you to move on. The folks that tell you that have never lost anyone so they don't realize that you don't get over the loss overnight. It blesses me to know and understand that God hurts when I hurt.

- God makes us confront the loss. This is where we don't fully understand how God works in our lives. God does not just pour salve into our wounds. God does not just

34

make things feel better. One of the ways God helps us heal is by making us confront what represents the pain. We would rather anesthetize and ignore the problem, but God does not let us escape into some ethereal world that doesn't deal with reality. God helps us confront our pain, which is something that we need to learn how to do. The reason Israel hadn't started rebuilding the temple was because they were still dealing with the pain of the loss of the temple. That is the same reason a lot of us haven't started rebuilding our lives, because we are still rocking and reeling from the pain and loss that brought us to where we are now.

GOD HELPS WITH
YOUR DISAPPOINTMENTS

God asked a simple question in Haggai chapter two: *"How does it look to you now?"* Our disappointment is often caused by how things look now. God made the children of Israel admit that they were disappointed in what had happened to the temple.

What that tells me is that you can do the best that you know to do and the end result will still be disappointment. You can give everything you have and come to the end, look around, and

Timothy J. Clarke

wonder, "Is this all I have to show for all I have done?"

Israel was dealing with disappointment. They looked at all of the work they had done only to realize that the new temple would be smaller, not as important, nor as beautiful as the original temple. Some of us have done the same thing. We do it with relationships. We give everything we have to something and then look at it and wonder, "Is this all?"

One of the hardest things to deal with is disappointment. I once talked with a pastor friend about a friendship that had gone sour. He and his friend were trying hard to reconcile their severed relationship, but my friend admitted that he didn't think the relationship would ever be the same. Even as he voiced his concerns it was not done out of arrogance or stubbornness, but with great disappointment. He realized that no matter how hard he worked at the relationship, the friendship was never going to be like it was before. What do you do when you have given your best and the end result doesn't measure up? You have to settle some things in your spirit:

- Some things cannot be changed. The day I realized that was when I knew I had grown up.

36

- Some things are beyond your control. There are some things that are not your fault, and while you don't deserve what happened (and it shouldn't have happened), the bottom line is it is beyond your control.

- Some things are the result of your decisions and they represent consequences. You can moan and groan and talk about how unfair life is, but if you are honest you will admit that some things you are dealing with are a result of your decisions and represent the consequences of those decisions. Israel was upset about how the temple looked because the other temple was destroyed, but the reason the other temple was destroyed was because God allowed the Babylonians to overthrow the city of Jerusalem because the people of God had rebelled against Him. If they had obeyed God, none of this would have happened. We reap what we sow, and many of the painful losses in our lives come as a result of decisions we have made.

GOD HELPS YOU ANTICIPATE YOUR FUTURE

You might be dealing with pain and disappointment, but God is working in your life not based on your losses, pain, and disappointments, but be-cause He sees your future:

> *This is what the Lord Almighty says: In a little while I will once more shake the heavens and the earth, the sea and the dry land. I will shake all nations, and the desired of all nations will come, and I will fill this house with glory, says the Lord Almighty.* (Haggai 2:6-7)

God gets excited about your future. You have had a lot of losses in your past and disappointments in your present, but thank God that where you have come from, and where you are now, is not where you are going! No matter the pain, loss, or disap-pointment, God has a plan for your future. You cannot get stuck in the quicksand of your yesterday looking back to what brought you pain. You cannot get stuck in the painful reality of your present because that brings you disappointment. What gives you hope when you wake up in the morning is that God has given you another chance.

"*In a little while*" does not mean that God will do something by a specific date, but what it speaks to is the inevitable move of God: He *is* going to move. God doesn't tell us when He is going to move, but we can rest assured that God is going to move. All you need to do is continue to praise, pray, fast, and seek God so that you are ready when the move of God occurs. What is coming for you is better than what has been. The God we serve is a God who is busy at work with us as we seek to rebuild our lives after something we love has been destroyed.

Chapter Five:
God Is Waiting On You

God expects us to roll up our sleeves and let Him use us to get the work done. We don't get to sit down, fold our arms, cross our legs, and let God do all the work.

King Darius had allowed all foreigners who had been taken as slaves to return to their home after years of exile. In Haggai chapter one the people had returned from captivity and was back in their homeland building houses for themselves, planting vineyards, reaping crops, and working in the field. The temple that was destroyed when the Babylonians sacked the city had not been rebuilt. The temple represented the center of their lives. It didn't matter what else they built, if that which represented their core was not in place, then their lives were not in order.

God wants us to do well and prosper; however, in our pursuit of the material things of life we must not deviate from that which represents our core: God. You can have houses, cars, money, and everything else, but if you don't have God, then when life turns on you—and it will—you won't be able to stand. That is the tragedy of so many people who started in the church, left the church, and then when life began to turn on them they had no frame of reference by which to ground themselves. When the shaking stops, the dust clears, and the smoke settles, all you will have is God.

In Haggai chapter one, God confronted His people about not rebuilding the temple. In chapter two, God counseled them and made them confront their loss, disappointment, and pain about the way the temple looked. Many of us are in relationships, marriages, careers and think that we should be further along. Rebuilding and restarting is never easy, but the reality is that none of us will get through life without several major rebuilding projects. You have to rebuild after having been laid off, or rebuild your finances after a foreclosure, or rebuild your health after sickness, or your self-image after a divorce, or rebuild your world after the death of a loved one. Whatever it is, none of us will get through life without having to be the fore-man, contractor, and architect of several major rebuilding projects. Some of you have your hard hat on right now because you are in the middle of a rebuilding project. I have good news for you which is crucial to rebuilding after something we love has been destroyed, so keep reading.

GOD WILL HELP YOU REBUILD,
BUT YOU MUST BE WILLING TO FORGET

When I was a child, I often heard preachers talk about forgiving and forgetting and it always sounded so easy until I got older. That is when I realized that forgiving and forgetting is easier said than done. Some of us are at a place in life where we need to rebuild, but we are stuck on the forgetting aspect of it. When I used to hear preachers say forgive and forget, I thought I would have this big eraser and I would just wipe the board clean. Forgetting does not mean that we can erase our memory, but it does mean we can choose how we will remember.

The Israelites chose to remember the past and wanted to live there. They remembered the glory and the splendor of the first temple and it kept them from engaging in the work of rebuilding a new temple. They were so stuck on how pretty the former temple was that they couldn't begin to focus on building a new temple.

It is like getting married after a certain age. Chances are that if you get married after the age of forty, you are most likely going to marry someone who has been married before. Either they are getting over a divorce or the death of a spouse. The challenge is that if they are coming out of a divorce, they are still hurting over the pain of that; if they

43

are coming out of the death of a spouse, they are hurting over the pain of that, and sometimes people want to live in the pain of the past. They cannot love a new person because they are still holding onto the past. You have to learn how not to live in your yesterday.

- Forgetting does not mean that you never look back. Sometimes you ought to take a glance back just for perspective and appreciation to realize how far you have come.

- Forgetting does not mean that you can't learn from the past. A lot of times we want to get out of the past so quickly that we don't learn the lessons of the past, which is why we continue to make the same mistakes.

- Forgetting means that you don't live in the past. You may view it and visit it, but you don't live there. Sometimes you look back just to thank God for where He has brought you from, and sometimes you look back to determine what you have learned.

GOD WILL HELP YOU REBUILD,
BUT YOU MUST STAY FOCUSED

Many times we can't make progress because we lose focus or we focus on the wrong things:

> *Be strong, all you people of the land, declares the Lord, and work. For I am with you, declares the Lord Almighty.* (Haggai 2:4(b))

A few months ago I had two projects at home: clean out the garage and clean out my closet. I didn't want to do either one. I had put them both off because the biggest challenge is knowing where to begin. There was so much to be done that I didn't even want to start, but once I did start I discovered that most of the boxes I needed to go through were empty. That told me that what looked like a lot of work was really not much work at all. Matter of fact, I finished quicker than I thought I would because I had lost my focus by being obsessed with the obvious and not applying myself to the task at hand.

A lot of times the enemy will make you believe that what you have to do is too much work, it is too hard, it takes too long when all you have to do is look and see that a lot of the stuff has already been done. You will discover that the task before

45

you is not that hard. What messed me up was that I was getting distracted by what looked like a lot of work.

- Focus is determined by what you pursue. If I am going to give my attention, effort, and time to something, I should ask myself what is the return on my investment? If you would ask yourself that, then you wouldn't get involved in a lot of stuff once you realized that you aren't going to get anything out of it.

- Focus is determined by what you permit. Whatever is going on in your life is what you have permitted. You could stop the madness right now because at some point you have developed a tolerance for whatever is going on. The only problem is that now that you have let the drama in it has become your focus and is absorbing all of your time, thoughts, and energy.

- Focus is determined by what you are passionate about. I pray to God that you are passionate about something. I could not imagine living a life devoid of passion. There should be something that excites you. It is scandalous for the saints of the Most High God to be dull, boring, and bland. That is a contradiction in terms. How can you serve a creative God and be dull? If He is creative, then you should be creative, too. I don't believe in boring saints. Something should ring your bell and get you excited.

GOD WILL HELP YOU REBUILD, BUT YOU MUST NOT FEAR

President Franklin D. Roosevelt, in his first inaugural address, said to a nation in the grip of a depression, "The only thing we have to fear is fear itself." But you and I know that fear itself can be foreboding; yet, the only way to make real progress is to face it and move on in spite of it. Courage is never the absence of fear, but the willingness to act even when you are afraid. I am sure if you were able to talk with any of the great martyrs, they would tell you that there were days they were afraid, but they acted in spite of the fear. God is with you and you don't have to fear.

You must learn to overcome your fear: *"...And my Spirit remains among you. Do not fear"* (Haggai 2:5(b)). How do you overcome fear? By giving God five more minutes to work.

There is a story told of two Civil War generals. Both sides were going back and forth in the battle; one side would win one day, the other side would win the next day. Finally the Union Army prevailed and when the winning general was interviewed, they asked him if he had won the battle because his men were braver, smarter, or stronger. The general responded, "No. We won that battle because my men were braver, smarter, stronger five minutes longer."

You only have five more minutes before your battle is over. If you will be braver and stronger five more minutes, God is going to step in and turn your situation around. Your five minutes may be five days, five weeks, five months, or five years, but if you hold onto God, He is going to show up, work it out, and fight your battle. God is going to give you the victory and bring you out. God is going to vindicate and deliver you. You just have to wait on the Lord.

PART THREE

GOD AT WORK
IN THE MIDST OF REBUILDING

Chapter Six:
Are You Up To The Challenge?

The Jews had returned home and life had taken on a rhythm of familiarity, but in the midst of making adjustments one thing was being neglected: The rebuilding of the temple that had been destroyed during the siege of the city.

One could almost argue that these people who had already endured so much could have been excused for wanting to get on with their lives and settling into what represented normalcy for them. After all, they had already suffered slavery, servitude, and subjugation so who could blame them for wanting to enjoy themselves. But God knew they would never be all they were called to be without the temple because the temple represented who they were: God's chosen people. Until the temple was in its proper place at the center of their lives, nothing they did would go right.

If God is not first in our lives, then nothing in our lives will go right either. You can have all the money, fame, and popularity, but without God at the center of your life, you are merely having an existence and not really living. Nothing takes the place of God in your life.

God will not live on the outskirts of our lives. If He is going to be in our lives, then He needs to be at the center of our lives. He must be first. This is what is wrong with a lot of us today. We want to put God in a place where He is not dangerous; where He doesn't get in our business or interfere in our affairs. But you are not smart enough or strong enough to handle things by yourself. If you are going to make it in this world, you need God in your life. If God is going to be in our lives, He must be front and center as the Lord of our lives. Some of you have placed your career, money, and friends first, but when the storm clouds gather your friends will flee, your money will go, and your popularity will die. But when everyone else walks out, God will walk in. When everyone else lets you down, God will lift you up. When everything else fails, God will still be there.

The task of rebuilding is never easy, and starting over is always more difficult than just starting. I understand to some degree what the children of Israel must have felt. We see how God allowed them to grieve over what they had lost and to face the disappointment of what they currently possessed. In His greatness, God did not leave them to languish in their pain or pity.

Some people like pain and some people enjoy pity. When Jesus asked the man who had sat by the pool for thirty-eight years if he wanted to be whole (John 5:1-15), on the surface it sounded like a silly question, but there are some people who don't want to get well because they enjoy the pity that comes with being sick. Sometimes a good kick in the shins is not the worst thing that can happen if the kick motivates us to go toward the path that God has set for us.

As you face the task of rebuilding something in your life that has all but been destroyed, you usually ask yourself a series of questions: Where do I start? What do I do first? Where do I begin? What makes rebuilding so challenging is that sometimes you don't even know where to begin. Contractors and architects will tell you that sometimes it is easier to build a new building than to refurbish an old one. That may also be true of a career, marriage, finances, or friendship. Putting things back together may be hard, but it will be worth the effort because what you rebuild will be prettier than anything you could have built if you had started new.

The work is hard; the task is daunting, the obstacles are many, and the risk is great but take heart: *"For I am with you, declares the Lord Almighty"* (Haggai 2:4). That is all you need to remember. No matter how long it takes, how hard the task; or how much rebuilding must be done, you can start now because God is with you.

GOD IS WITH YOU MANIFESTING HIS POWER

What blesses and comforts me are the dimensions and scope of God's power. Some of you didn't grow up attending Church or Sunday school and have no frame of reference for who God is. Even though I told you He was with you, if you don't know who He is, then you can't get excited about that. The God that is with you is the Awesome El Elyon, the Most High God:

> *This is what the Lord Almighty says: In a little while I will once more shake the heavens and the earth, the sea and the dry land. I will shake all nations, and the desired of all nations will come, and I will fill this house with glory, says the Lord Almighty.* (Haggai 2:6-7)

Everything you can see in the sky is under God's power. Everything you need a telescope or a Hubble to see is under God's power. But what the Hubble can't capture and what the satellites can't pick up; what the astronauts have never seen is the third heaven where angels bow before Him and heaven and earth adore Him in the rarefied atmosphere of the heavens of the heavens of the heavens. God says He has power right there. He talks about shaking the heaven and the earth, which is this world order. Shaking the earth means that all of the people are under His power. He talks about the sea and the dry land, which means that all of the animals, mammals, everything swimming under the sea, and all of the things under the ground belong to Him. So since God owns all of that, what are you worried about?

GOD IS WITH YOU MAKING KNOWN HIS PROVISION

The children of Israel were reluctant to begin the task of rebuilding because they realized the new temple would not be as extravagant as the original one. That is why God reminded them that He had whatever they needed: *"The silver is mine and the gold is mine, declares the Lord Almighty,"* (Haggai 2:8).

God is reminding you of the same thing: Whatever you need, God has it. God spoke of the silver and the gold which are the things the economy is based on. If you run out of money and have God, He can still supply all of your needs. He allows you to be blessed in the midst of your storm.

GOD IS WITH YOU MINISTERING HIS PEACE

The Hebrew word for peace is *shalom*, which means nothing broken, nothing lacking, nothing missing:

> *The glory of this present house will be greater than the glory of the former house, says the Lord Almighty. And in this place I will grant peace, declares the Lord Almighty.* (Haggai 2:9)

I wish you would embrace your future and get excited about what is coming. Remember I told you about the splendor of Solomon's temple? There came a point that because of Solomon's lifestyle he lost the favor of God and the people of God began to turn away from God. They had a pretty building, but there wasn't any power in it. God said that the new house (temple) might not be as pretty as Solomon's, but the glory in the house would make the house greater than Solomon's.

You might not have as much as you used to have, but you have something now that you didn't have before. You have the peace of God. You have the joy of God. Peace and joy that the world didn't give and the world can't take away.

Chapter Seven:
Don't You Care About Me?

Leadership is one of the most crucial things in the life of a nation, a church, and a community. Everyone suffers when leadership is not in place or the leadership is not led by God. We can never dismiss or discount the role of leadership in our lives. When you suffer under poor leadership, you always feel the damaging effects of it. The opposite is true, too. When you are under a good leader, you always experience the blessing of good leadership. I am trying to get you to understand that leadership is vital to our success in life. Whether it is leadership at work or home; in the community or in the nation, leaders must function under the anointing and power of God. There is a blessing from being under good leadership.

Our families rise and fall on leadership. That is one of the reasons why the Church must always challenge our men to step to the plate when it comes to their role in the family. That does not discount the value of women or diminish the role of the mother, but I think that all of us can acknowledge that there is something about the presence of a man in a family that makes a tremendous difference. A wife should be excited that she has a husband who is a good provider for her even though he is not perfect. A husband should be excited that his wife puts up with him even though she is not perfect. A child should be excited that their parents take care of them even though they are not perfect.

Leadership in the Church should not be taken for granted either. If God blesses a church with a good leader, that church should celebrate the leader, thank God for the leader, and then follow the leader. The reason I can say that is because God has blessed me for over thirty years to pastor a church that has never given me trouble, never fought, resisted, or rebelled against me. I am trying to get you to understand that when God gives you a good leader, you should be thankful for the leader God has given you.

It is the same with public servants, whether you voted for them or not. If they are providing leadership to your city, community, state or nation, then thank God that you have leaders who are not afraid to lead.

A MAN COMFORTABLE IN HIS OWN SKIN

One of my favorite Bible characters is Nehemiah, who literally personifies what it means to be a good leader. He was not a priest, prophet, or preacher; yet, God used him in a powerful way.

You should get excited about that because what that means is you don't have to be in the pulpit to be used of God. You don't have to buy a robe, wear a turned around collar, attend seminary, or any of those things. All you have to do is make yourself available so that God can use you right where you are, the way you are. Sometimes the Church is guilty of perpetuating the myth that the only anointed ones are sitting in the pulpit. Some of you may agree with that so you can continue to sit in the pew and not hold to your measure of responsibility. My job is to make you aware that you don't have to be a preacher to be used of God. If the work of the Kingdom is going to get done, the pulpit cannot do it all. God doesn't just use preachers to get His work done; we are in this together. Leadership is not just in the pulpit; it is among God's people. While there are levels of authority, there is only one pastor who is responsible before God for a congregation. That is not to say that others aren't anointed because all of us are gifted to do something for the glory of God.

AN IDEAL RELATIONSHIP

When you read the Book of Nehemiah, you will discover a priest named Ezra. What blesses me is how well Ezra and Nehemiah got along. Ezra knew his place; Nehemiah knew his place and both of them stayed in their place.

The city you live in has a mayor, the chief of police, and the city council; everybody has a role, but in order for them to be effective they have to stay in their lane of anointing:

> *Early the following spring, in the month of Nisan, during the twentieth year of King Artaxerxes' reign, I was serving the king his wine. I had never before appeared sad in his presence. So the king asked me, "Why are you looking so sad? You don't look sick to me. You must be deeply troubled." Then I was terrified, but I replied, "Long live the king! How can I not be sad? For the city where my ancestors are buried is in ruins, and the gates have been destroyed by fire." The king asked, "Well, how can I help you?" With a prayer to the God of heaven, I replied, "If it please the king, and if you are pleased with me, your servant, send me to Judah to rebuild the city where my an-*

*cestors are buried." The king, with the
queen sitting beside him, asked, "How
long will you be gone? When will you return?" After I told him how long I would
be gone, the king agreed to my request.*
(Nehemiah 2:1-6, NLT)

In biblical times, walls represented the safety and
identity of a city. After fifty years of the people
returning home and not rebuilding the wall, God
chose Nehemiah to get the work done. When Israel
was facing the result of the wall of Jerusalem being
torn down, God raised up Nehemiah and sent him
to go back to work on the rebuilding of the wall.

    There was no competition between Nehemiah
and Ezra and that is the way the Church should be.
The clergy can't be jealous of the laity and vice
versa. We are not in competition but workers
together. Can you imagine what would happen if we
would stop fighting one another and learn how to
work together instead of tearing one another down?
Both Nehemiah and Ezra understood who they were
and that they each had a role to play in the Kingdom. When it was time to build and lay bricks, Ezra
sat down; when it was time to preach, Nehemiah
sat down. There was no confusion about their roles,
which was why there was no competition. That is a
valuable life lesson, not just a spiritual lesson.
Everything is not a race. Everything is not about

winning or losing. Some things are just about getting the job done.

Years ago I heard Pastor Chuck Swindoll tell a story about former President Jimmy Carter. He was watching President Carter make a speech from the Oval Office and he noticed a plaque on his desk and wondered what it said. Pastor Swindoll called the White House and asked the operator. The operator didn't know because she had never been in the Oval Office. He asked her to find out and she asked several people before she got in touch with Mr. Carter's personal secretary. The operator told the secretary why she was calling; the secretary went into the office and came back and told her what the plaque said: "It is amazing what can get done when people don't care who takes the credit."

If that works in the Oval Office, I know it will work in the Kingdom because the bottom line is that when people get saved, blessed, and have their lives changed, the glory doesn't come to us but to God. That is the problem with some of our churches; we have too many people squabbling over who will get the credit rather than God getting the glory.

God used Nehemiah and Ezra to accomplish something great for the Kingdom. Nothing great can be done by one person. You can build a chicken coop by yourself, but not a skyscraper. You can build a doghouse by yourself, but not a mansion.

You can build a shanty by yourself, but not a palace. You can build a room by yourself, but not a cathedral. You really can't do anything great for God by yourself. It takes all of us putting our best foot forward to accomplish something great because we need each other.

AND THE WALLS WENT UP

God raised up Nehemiah because there was a problem in Jerusalem: the walls were torn down and the gates were burned. Torn down walls might not mean anything to us because our cities don't have walls around them. But in biblical times a wall around the city indicated where the city started and ended, its occupants, and the city limits. For a city not to have walls meant it was vulnerable and exposed.

Many of us have had the walls of our lives damaged by things that were supposed to protect us and give us a sense of identity and security. You may feel vulnerable because some walls in your life have been damaged. You are able to look through a hole in some emotional or relational wall of your life and begin to feel unsure, uncertain, and unsafe. When the wall was whole, you felt invincible. When the wall was solid, you felt secure. Now the remaining sections of the walls are more of an insult than if the whole wall was gone because the wall only

63

serves to remind you of how good, how strong, how secure it used to be. Something or someone has damaged the walls of your life.

We all need walls that give us security and identity, but we must be very careful about the walls we put up. Your house, job, money, or reputation can't be your walls because those things will fail and then you will lose your sense of identity. However, when you build your life on God, then no matter what you lose, you will still know who you are because of your relationship with Him.

Fifty years after Darius allowed the Jews to return to their homeland they still had not rebuilt the walls, apparently content to be surrounded by unsecured walls. One day Nehemiah was walking through the city in Susa and heard a familiar dialect. He inquired about the people back home and was told that things were not good. God used Nehemiah to make a change and he becomes a prototype of the type of people God still looks for today:

- People who are broken. Not people who are broke, but those who are broken. When Nehemiah heard the condition of his people, he wept and sobbed uncontrollably. No rebuilding project begins until a person is broken and the current condition is no longer tolerable. Until you are broken over what is going on you will never change the conditions. The current reality has to become intolerable.

- People who are burdened. Once God breaks you, He is then able to put a burden on you about somebody else's future. Burdens don't come to people who are not broken and who don't care. Once you allow God to break you, then you will put yourself in a place, posture, and position where God can burden you. That is when the real change comes. When something weighs on you so heavily that things are no longer cute or funny, you walk around with a sense that something has to change whether it's in your relationships, community, finances, health, career, or walk with God. After you are broken, then begins the burden. God uses men and women to rebuild after He breaks them. I wonder how many Christians have allowed God to break us so He can use us.

- People who are willing to go back. Nehemiah lived and worked in Susa, the capital of Persia. He was the cupbearer to the king, which is similar to being a member of the President's cabinet. Nehemiah had done well for himself and he was a long way removed from Jerusalem with its torn down walls. But when the news came about his people in Jerusalem, God broke him and burdened him and he could not stay where he was. He sensed a call to go back to Jerusalem. And God may want to send you back, too, to help someone else. Everybody you know is not doing well and God may want to use you to help them. Somebody needs to hear what God has done for you. Somebody needs to know that if God helped you, He can help them, too.

Walls can be rebuilt if you just let God use you. You have to go back because there are people who need what you have. They need somebody to tell them that it doesn't matter what they have done, God is able to rebuild the damaged areas of their lives.

Chapter Eight:
Let the Celebration Begin

There are times when the walls of our lives are damaged and we feel defenseless and vulnerable. If the walls of our lives have been damaged, the God we serve is a God who masters in rebuilding and repairing broken walls. It doesn't matter what happened or where the damage came from, God is able to rebuild the walls. Who does God use when He is rebuilding the walls of our lives?

GOD USES PEOPLE WHO WORK

The walls of Jerusalem didn't go up by magic; the people had to work:

> But now I said to them, "You know full well the tragedy of our city. It lies in ruins, and its gates are burned. Let us rebuild the wall of Jerusalem and rid ourselves of this disgrace!" Then I told them about how the gracious hand of God had been on me, and about my conversation with the king. They replied at

> *once, "Good! Let's rebuild the wall!" So*
> *they began the good work.* (Nehemiah
> 2:17-18, NLT)

If you are going to see results and reap a harvest, you have to work. You should be standing on the promises and not sitting on the premises. Faith without works is dead (James 2:20). Show me your faith and I will show you my works by my faith. I work because I have faith and I know that if I work, God will work with and for me. God will do what I cannot do. If you want your walk with God to be richer, deeper, fuller, then you have to work at it. Nothing comes without work.

Where does the work ethic come from? From the desire to want something more, the discipline to do what needs to be done, and the diligence to keep working in spite of what else may be going on.

GOD USES PEOPLE WHO WAR

Nehemiah utilized ambidextrous people who could work with a hammer in one hand and a sword in the other. If their enemies came against them, that wasn't the time to pray. They were to put down the hammer and pick up the sword:

> *When our enemies heard that we knew of*
> *their plans and that God had frustrated*

them, we all returned to our work on the wall. But from then on, only half my men worked while the other half stood guard with spears, shields, bows, and coats of mail. The officers stationed themselves behind the people of Judah who were building the wall. The common laborers carried on their work with one hand supporting their load and one hand holding a weapon. All of the builders had a sword belted to their side. The trumpeter stayed with me to sound the alarm. (Nehemiah 4:15-18, NLT)

There is a time to fight. *"There is a time for everything, and a season for every activity under heaven...a time for war and a time for peace"* (Ecclesiastes 3:1(a), 8(b)). One of the keys in life is knowing when to fight. I am not talking about a physical fight; I am talking about taking a stand. That is part of the problem with our world today. We don't stand for anything. We are very wishy-washy; we have no convictions and no strong faith.

Some things are worth the risk. Dr. Martin Luther King, Jr. once said, "I am deeply disappointed in America, but the only reason I am disappointed in America is because I love America. There can be no great disappointment where there is not great love."

69

Like Dr. King, I, too, love America, but that doesn't mean I am unaware of the ills and equity of this country. With the current economic crisis and challenges facing us; the divisiveness that has become normal, and the vitriolic nature of our political discourse, America is still the risk. We are a great nation, and our greatness is equal to our goodness.

<u>When it is time to fight, you better fight to win</u>. You don't go into a fight with a gorilla carrying a fly swatter. When you know it is time to fight, and you have found something worth fighting for, then fight to win. You may not win every time, but I have discovered that if you go in it to win it, God will help you.

GOD IS AT WORK AMONG PEOPLE WHO WORSHIP

When the work was finished and the wall was rebuilt, they gathered to worship:

> *During the dedication of the new wall of Jerusalem, the Levites throughout the land were asked to come to Jerusalem to assist in the ceremonies. They were to take part in the joyous occasion with their songs of thanksgiving and with the*

music of cymbals, lyres and harps. . .The priests and Levites first dedicated themselves, then the people, the gates, and the wall. . .Many sacrifices were offered on that joyous day, for God had given the people cause for great joy. The women and children also participated in the celebration, and the joy of the people of Jerusalem could be heard far away. (Nehemiah 12:27, 30, 43, NLT)

I know people look at the members of my church and say, "See, that's why I don't go to church because they're loud, uncouth, and rowdy." My only problem with that statement is that those same people will go to an Ohio State football game and get loud, uncouth, and rowdy, but they want to talk about us because we are praising the God of our salvation. There was a time when I used to feel bad and tried to tone down my praise because I didn't want someone to think I was loud, uncouth, and rowdy. But then I started thinking about how good God has been to me and I determined that the devil was a liar; if people can shout over the Ohio State Buckeyes and other sports teams, then God knows I can shout over the goodness of God in my life!

Praise is our secret weapon. When the devil backs me into a corner, I reach into my bag and pull out some praise. When I start praising God, I

71

know something is about to happen. If you are going through a struggle, you can be pitiful or you can start praising. You can be sad or you can start shouting. You can be depressed or you can start dancing. I choose to bless the Lord and let His praise be continually in my mouth:

> *Now in midautumn, when the Israelites had settled in their towns, all the people assembled together as one person at the square just inside the Water Gate. They asked Ezra the scribe to bring out the Book of the Law of Moses, which the Lord had given for Israel to obey. . .Then Nehemiah the governor, Ezra the priest and scribe, and the Levites who were interpreting for the people said to them, "Don't weep on such a day as this! For today is a sacred day before the Lord your God." All the people had been weeping as they listened to the words of the law.* (Nehemiah 8:1, 9, NLT)

When the Word of God was being read, the realized how long it had been since they had actually *heard* God's Word. They begin to weep and mourn, but Ezra reminded them that it was not a day for weeping; it was a day for rejoicing because the joy of the Lord was their strength.

Perhaps you have cried long enough and it is time for you to start rejoicing. Remember I told you in chapter one that the prefix "re" means to go back to your original state, so rejoicing means to go back to your joy. When God brings you out, you won't come out dragging and sad, but shouting and rejoicing because God will have given you plenty of reasons to be grateful.

Has God made a way for you? Has God opened doors for you? Has God healed your body? Has God brought down your mountains and raised up your valleys? Has God put food on your table, clothes on your back, and gas in your car? Has God made a way out of no way? Any and all of those are reasons enough to praise Him!

The God we serve does His best work behind the scenes and is working when you and I are unaware of what is going on. The unseen hand of God is working in your situation, your condition and your problem. In fact, He gave you the problem so that you could see how good He is, and how much God He is, so that when He works it out, all of the glory, honor, and praise goes to Him. You may not be able to see Him, or understand what He is doing or why, but you need to hold onto Romans 8:28 (NLT):

> *And we know that God causes everything to work together for the good of those who love God and are called according to His purpose for them.*

One of the things the devil will try to make you believe is that God has abandoned or forsaken you, especially when you are going through trying times, but the Word of God says, *"Never will I leave you; never will I forsake you,"* (Hebrews 13:5).

Beloved, I want to remind you that in the midst of whatever you are going through, you can rest in the calming assurance of *Caution! God at*

Work. God is with you and He is working on your behalf.

Please enjoy this excerpt from *Reclaim Your Spiritual Health*, ISBN 978-0-9764022-3-7:

God is the Habit Breaker. It doesn't matter how long you have had a habit or how deep the habit has become ingrained in you. If you come to Jesus, He is able to step into your addiction, loose you, and set you free. You know that whom the Son sets free is free indeed (John 8:36). You must also remember to contend for the faith (Jude 3) and to stand in the liberty in which Christ has set you free (Galatians 5:1). In other words you must maintain your freedom and deliverance.

This is where a lot of people mess up. They are set free and assume that is all they have to do. Once you are free you have to fight to stay free. Once the Lord sets you free the devil keeps on coming at you. If you stand your ground, hold on, and fight the good fight of faith, you can maintain your freedom.

One of the ways that happens is with the Twelve Steps. It helps many to stand firm in their recovery. You cannot spend a lifetime of getting into something and think that a twenty minute emotional encounter is all that it is going to take to get you out. It will take more than that.

You must realize that your struggles don't just affect you; they affect other people. It is never just about you and it doesn't end with just you. That is why you must take inventory of your life and admit that while trying to balance career and family, success and salvation, things sometimes get out of control. So how do you get control back?

<u>Focus on a few things rather than everything</u>. You can't do it all. Do you know people who run from one thing to another? Every time you meet them, they are doing something new. That is what Solomon did:

> *I wanted to see what was worthwhile for men to do under heaven during the few days of their lives. I undertook great projects; I built houses for myself and planted vineyards. I made gardens and parks and planted all kinds of fruit trees in them. I made reservoirs to water groves of flourishing trees. I bought male and female slaves and had other slaves who were born in my house. I also owned more herds and flocks than anyone in Jerusalem before me. I amassed silver and gold for myself, and the treasure of kings*

and provinces. I acquired men and women singers, and a harem as well—the delights of the heart of man. I became greater by far than anyone in Jerusalem before me. (Ecclesiastes 2:3-9)

Solomon discovered what you will discover: You will never be happy until you narrow your focus. You can't do it all. Sit down and get a clear vision of what it is you want to do with your life. Where do you want to be in two years? Five years? Ten years? What is your vision? Watch what you run after. There is an old proverb that says that any man who chases two rabbits at the same time will miss them both. Decide which rabbit you are going after.

<u>Focus on what you were meant to do</u>. Philippians 3:13 has the Apostle Paul referring to *". . . this one thing I do. . ."*

Do you know how to separate successful people from mediocre people? Successful people have determined the "one thing" they do. Michael Jordan is Michael Jordan because he focused on basketball. Tiger Woods is Tiger Woods because he focuses on golf. I was born to pastor First Church of God in Columbus, Ohio. In fact all that I do of any consequence comes out of being the Senior Pastor of First Church. Any books I write, any speaking I do, any impact I have is because I have focused my life on First Church of God. I am happy and excited because I am doing what I was created to do.

You are no different. Your life will never be what it should be until you can say like the apostle, *". . . this one thing I do. . ."* You may be able to do several things, but you were meant to do one thing.

<u>Focus on eternity, not immediacy</u>. Most of what Solomon did was for instant gratification, immediate pleasure, and imminent happiness.

You have to stop living like today is the only day you are ever going to have. If you want to live in the long term, ask yourself:

- What am I creating? What kind of home? What kind of children? What kind of relationships with family, friends, and God? What kind of financial future?

- What am I giving? What am I giving to my family and others? What am I giving to God and the Kingdom?

- What am I leaving behind? From here on out it is all about legacy. Steven Covey in *Seven Habits of Highly Effective People* encourages us to begin with the end in mind. If you should die tonight, what would the preacher say is your legacy? What would friends, family, and saints say about you? What would God say about you?

Step one of the Twelve Steps says that, "We admit we are powerless and our lives have become unmanageable." For many of you that is where you are. Like Solomon you are looking for what can only be found in God. It is only when you turn your life over to Him that your life will make sense. A verse from the song, *Only What You Do for Christ Will Last* by Raymond Rasberry, says it best:

> You can build great cathedrals large and small.
> You can build skyscrapers grand and tall.
> You can conquer all the failures of your past.
> But only what you do for Christ will last.
> Only what you do for Him will be counted in the end.
> Only what you do for Christ will last.

Other Books by
Bishop Timothy J. Clarke

Caution: God at Work – Trusting God through tough times

Celebrating the Family: Lessons from the Book of Ruth

Living in the Blessed Place

Making the Most of Your Time

The Price of Victory: Strategies for winning a faith fight

Reclaim Your Spiritual Health

To My Sisters Beloved: A trilogy of encouragement